# NOTES FROM AND ABOUT COACHING COLLEGE RUGBY

YA GOTTA BUY THE T-SHIRT

# NOTES FROM AND ABOUT COACHING COLLEGE RUGBY

### YA GOTTA BUY THE T-SHIRT

William Laughlin "Loc" Vetter, M.D., FACS

**PALMETTO**
**P U B L I S H I N G**
Charleston, SC
www.PalmettoPublishing.com

Copyright © 2024 by William Laughlin "Loc" Vetter, M.D., FACS

All rights reserved.

No portion of this book may be reproduced, stored in a retrieval system, or transmitted in any form by any means–electronic, mechanical, photocopy, recording, or other–except for brief quotations in printed reviews, without prior permission of the author.

Paperback ISBN: 979-8-8229-5641-4
eBook ISBN: 979-8-8229-5808-1

*To the countless coaches, players, parents, unsolicited suggestors, and teachers who have impacted this content, with whom I've been blessed and to whom I am forever grateful.*

# CONTENTS

Preface · · · · · · · · · · · · · · · · · · · · · · · · · · · · · · · · · ix
Notes from and about Coaching College Rugby
    Introduction · · · · · · · · · · · · · · · · · · · · · · · · · · · xi
Gender Neutrality · · · · · · · · · · · · · · · · · · · · · · · · · · · 1
T-shirt Principles · · · · · · · · · · · · · · · · · · · · · · · · · · · 2
College Players Need to Know Why · · · · · · · · · · · · · · · 5
You Cannot Make Shit Shine · · · · · · · · · · · · · · · · · · · · 8
Why College Rugby? · · · · · · · · · · · · · · · · · · · · · · · · · 9
To Ruck or to Maul in the College Game · · · · · · · · · · 11
Most Basic Things and Encouraging Questions · · · · 13
Pass the Ball Straight Across the Field · · · · · · · · · · · 15
Near Touch, Use the Outside Shoulder · · · · · · · · · · 18
No Bad Passes · · · · · · · · · · · · · · · · · · · · · · · · · · · · 19
Tuck Your Ears · · · · · · · · · · · · · · · · · · · · · · · · · · · · 20
Bend Your Knees · · · · · · · · · · · · · · · · · · · · · · · · · · 22
Run Straight Up field · · · · · · · · · · · · · · · · · · · · · · · 24
Unify the Construct · · · · · · · · · · · · · · · · · · · · · · · · 26
Explode the Tackle · · · · · · · · · · · · · · · · · · · · · · · · · 28
Never punch the ground · · · · · · · · · · · · · · · · · · · · · 30
Skills at Pace · · · · · · · · · · · · · · · · · · · · · · · · · · · · · 32

Get to Your Blocks · · · · · · · · · · · · · · · · · · · · · · · · 33
Play on the Boil · · · · · · · · · · · · · · · · · · · · · · · · · · 35
Chin off Your Chest · · · · · · · · · · · · · · · · · · · · · · · 37
Two Hands on the Ball · · · · · · · · · · · · · · · · · · · · · 38
Dive out of the Pool · · · · · · · · · · · · · · · · · · · · · · 39
Double Bounce Try · · · · · · · · · · · · · · · · · · · · · · · 40
Show Glee after Tries · · · · · · · · · · · · · · · · · · · · · 41
Kick to Ourselves or to Touch · · · · · · · · · · · · · · · 42
Call for the Ball · · · · · · · · · · · · · · · · · · · · · · · · · · 45
NEVER Let the High ball Bounce · · · · · · · · · · · · 47
Better Late · · · · · · · · · · · · · · · · · · · · · · · · · · · · · · 48
Practice with Perfection · · · · · · · · · · · · · · · · · · · 49
Don't Lose the F Ball · · · · · · · · · · · · · · · · · · · · · 51
Not just "With You" · · · · · · · · · · · · · · · · · · · · · · 52
Slacken, Shorten, Straighten, Swerve/Shoot, Sprint · 53
Juice Ball to the Wing · · · · · · · · · · · · · · · · · · · · 55
Ball's Out! · · · · · · · · · · · · · · · · · · · · · · · · · · · · · · 57
Lama Lama! · · · · · · · · · · · · · · · · · · · · · · · · · · · · · 58
You Gotta Buy the T-Shirt · · · · · · · · · · · · · · · · · 59
Survivor to Player · · · · · · · · · · · · · · · · · · · · · · · · 61
Stack Memory · · · · · · · · · · · · · · · · · · · · · · · · · · · 64
Coaches in Cahoots and Halftime Housekeeping · · 66
Ecclesiastes 9:10 · · · · · · · · · · · · · · · · · · · · · · · · · 68
Class Act · · · · · · · · · · · · · · · · · · · · · · · · · · · · · · · 69
Spiderman · · · · · · · · · · · · · · · · · · · · · · · · · · · · · · 71
Remembering · · · · · · · · · · · · · · · · · · · · · · · · · · · 72
Dr. Arnold Beisser · · · · · · · · · · · · · · · · · · · · · · · · 73
Final thought · · · · · · · · · · · · · · · · · · · · · · · · · · · · 77

# PREFACE

Even if you have never seen rugby played, this little book will enrich you. Not so much because you need to know the difference between a ruck and a maul, but rather because learning of team play is learning of a ubiquitous element of our society and personal relationships.

"Ya Gotta Buy the T-shirt," is a piecemeal presentation of true and valuable tidbits. That there is value to each member of a team, agreeing to do skills for which there are several options in one way, is just plain true. Knowing what one another are going to do makes people and teams better. The notion that opponents are put on-notice is helpful to our goal of winning, in games and in life.

Not every point made here is spot on and timely. Indeed, coming to agreement should include assessment of options and deciding which might be best for your team. What an enriching exercise!

# NOTES FROM AND ABOUT COACHING COLLEGE RUGBY
# INTRODUCTION

The intent of this manifesto is to share, provide topics for thought, and kindle conversation. Over the course of approximately 22 years coaching rugby, mostly with 15-player college teams, there have been options chosen that appeared to improve both success and enjoyment. These "options" included rugby skills and techniques, coaching style, and a cultivated team attitude. Where I was privileged to coach there were typically fall and spring seasons each year. The nature of the beast was that there were many new players at the starts of these 40+ seasons. Therefore, all of this has been tried to at least that extent. Of course, one adjusts according to the players gathered for a particular season. We might take advantage of a talented kicker or an exceptional redrive runner, but generally here I am selecting options that have proven effective for all our teams. By utilizing these strategies, we not only achieved success, but also improved as players, coaches, and individuals.

No doubt, some people would disagree with at least some of the principles presented here. Good, as the nature of techniques used decades ago is that many of them may no longer be best practices. A hope of mine is that thoughts and discussions will be kindled.

I apologize for not being able to properly credit those from whom I learned almost all of this. Memory just does not serve. Some people come fondly to mind. My first coach was Dennis Storer, Loughborough trained and first Eagle coach. Among so many others were: Jack Clark, Dr. Harvey Zarins, Dr. Dale Toohey, Mike Flanagan, Dan Porter, Ron Mayes, Ray Cornbill, Jimmy Parker, Skip Niebauer, Pete Steinberg, Steve Gray, Bing Dawson, Hugh Anderson, Divan Serfontein, Bill Freeman, and Dr. Arnold Beisser. There have been so many more. I no doubt picked up things from my high school teachers and coaches. There were 17 years between receiving my high school diploma and hanging up my shingle as an orthopedic surgeon, I had many mentors. Some small fraction of what is here might be original, including some coaching style points. If something does not work for you, it was probably mine and therefore, if it does not work for you, it is my fault.

This pamphlet will meander within a topic and skip from one to another aspect of the game as the discussion progresses. How to execute a sidestep may be followed by body position in support of a teammate at the breakdown. Such is this complex hodgepodge of a game. Some topics warrant more comments than others. Yea, brevity!

I cover a couple of points twice, which is emphasis of importance over brevity.

There are already well-written, comprehensive guides to the game. Books like "Rugby Simplified," "Rugby for Dummies," and "Thinking Rugby" are examples. Here, I am presenting my personal choices regarding the elements I consider important. It is not meant to be read cover to cover, but rather to be picked up, opened, and whatever is there contemplated. It is unlikely that someone could read this pamphlet and then go play rugby. In addition to this manifesto, aspiring players looking to improve will have to learn by:

- Watching
- Being thrown into the thick of it
- Solitary contemplation
- Being coached
- Reading
- Reading the Laws of the Game (very rarely done)
- Experiencing "Oo-that-didn't-work"
- Discussions, dark-of-night-cold-of-beer
- Being shown how it is done
- Being played against
- Stuff of dreams
- Tribal Learning
- Losing

# GENDER NEUTRALITY

Except when writing about a specific person, there are no gender-specific pronouns used here. In this booklet, there is an emphasis on the importance of team concepts and playing rugby as a cohesive unit. It is grammatically impossible for the noun "team" to be used as the antecedent for any of the seven gender-specific pronouns.

Team pronouns: When preparing talks for inductions to Halls of Fame, I read what the inductees had written in response to their notifications. There was not a single "I," "me," or "my." All used only "we," "us," or "our." While certainly they did feel personally honored, their expressed thoughts were purely team.

# T-SHIRT PRINCIPLES

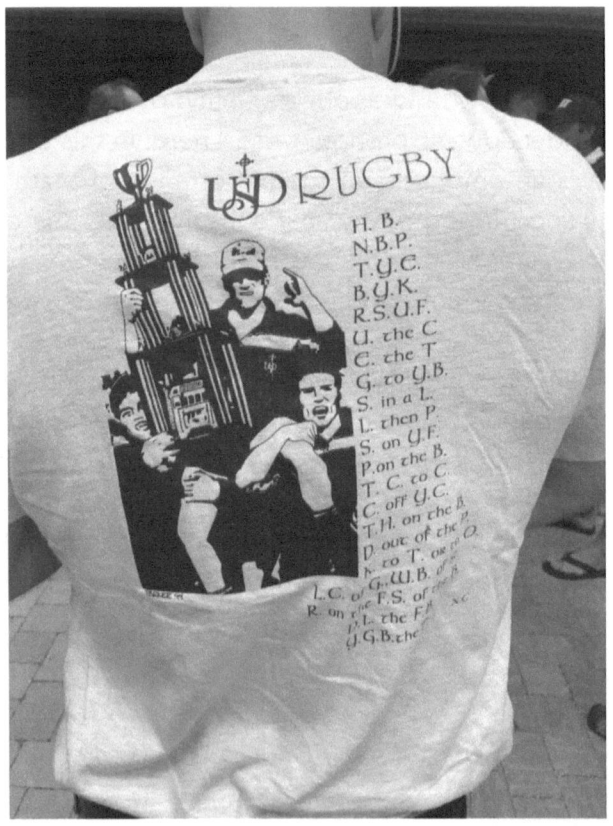

In the middle of my coaching life, it was noticed that players and the coaches, including myself, were frequently using certain catchphrases. Maybe I had harped on them too much. After winning a Las Vegas tournament, defeating Camp Pendleton in the finals (professional warriors who stay fit for a living), a cool photo of celebration was incorporated into a team shirt.

The initials on this shirt are for:

- Head Behind
- No Bad Passes
- Tuck Your Ears
- Bend Your Knees
- Run Straight Up the field
- Unify the Construct
- Explode the Tackle
- Get to Your Blocks
- Spine in a Line
- Look then Pass
- Stay on your Feet
- Play on the Boil
- Chin off Your Chest
- Two Hands on the Ball
- Dive out of the Pool
- Kick to Ourselves, or to Touch
- Low Center of Gravity Wide base of support
- Ruck on the Far Side of the Ball
- Don't Lose the F Ball
- You Gotta Buy the T-Shirt

Not on the shirt but perhaps should have been:

- Use teammates' names
- Pass the Ball Straight Across the Field
- Slacken, Shorten, Straighten, Swerve/Shoot, Sprint
- Quick Ball to the Wing
- Call for the Ball
- Ball's Out

When everyone on the team is playing with the same set of options for how our game should be played, including the game plan, techniques, and tactics, it fosters a synergy that is genuinely enhancing and enjoyable. This unity among teammates leads to a sense of camaraderie, as they collectively embrace "our game" and relish in sharing victories.

Recalling anything on this list and thinking slightly beyond the box: whether it is sales, finance, medicine, law, religion, engineering, real estate, entrepreneurship, public service, or politics — these principles are relevant.

So, teaching points, mantras, items on a checklist, dichos, metaphors, aphorisms, adages, or whatever you want to call them, these are applicable to life beyond sport.

Some of these are self-explanatory or implicitly clear. Those that are not will be further explained here.

# COLLEGE PLAYERS NEED TO KNOW WHY

Coaches,

Do not expect college athletes to accept anything simply because you say it is or should be so. If you don't sell it, they won't buy it. These are professional learners. Many are, for the first time in their lives, making decisions independently of their parents. They are encouraged in the college experience to develop and exercise their freedom of choice.

Example: It is not at all obvious to a kid new to the game that when making a tackle, a good place for their cheek is on the opponent's butt. But, when explained that if you tackle cheek to cheek, you press your facial cheek to their butt cheek, good things happen:

- It puts your head behind and likely your center of gravity lower than your opponent's. More importantly, ...
- If the ball carrier is running forward, they are likely to fall forward. If you are on the back side, you will end up on top, allowing you to get to your feet and back into play first.
- Most importantly, it is very difficult to be punched, kicked, kneed, or elbowed when you have your cheek glued to someone's butt. It is the safest place for your head to be.
- As a corollary, the next time you are told you have your head up your butt, you can respond by saying, "Yes, and it is very safe."

An anecdote: At an after-match for a game that we had won solidly a young man approached me and, with impaired speech due to alcohol, expressed his belief: "You coach a dirty game." Well, that burst my bubble! I left the party. I stewed. Called some friends whose opinions I respected. The message: When necessary, reassess your actions, particularly when advised to do so, even by a drunk. After careful study of this case, it was found that the young man's head was remarkably safe, as it was not just on, but up his butt.

Optionally, I might have quipped, "Oh, were you there? I didn't notice you."

# YOU CANNOT MAKE SHIT SHINE

You cannot make every player an All-American or each team a National Champion, but you and your players always enrich one another.

It is true, as a plastic surgeon friend once explained, "You can rub it and rub it and rub it, but you can't make shit shine." However, every player deserves your best effort as a coach, each player and the team will benefit.

# WHY COLLEGE RUGBY?

At a gathering a few years ago, I listened to a group of intelligent, experienced, educated, and articulate rugby players explain to one another what it is that is special about college rugby. I found their words, while heartfelt, just did not quite resonate with me.

Yes, cherished memories, brotherhood, and a sense of belonging are important, but I feel there is more to it.

At that gathering I wasn't ready to stand and opine. Instead, I went home and attempted to write down my thoughts on "Why college rugby?" After completing a draft, I sent it to Jack Clark. He liked it, but generously gave me this added concept: Higher education is done alone. Think about it: choosing a major, going to class, studying, and reading—the very essence of graded college learning is done alone. The problems of the world that need solving will require a team approach. Rugby is inescapably, inherently, quintessentially a team experience.

Whether it's family, profession, church, citizenship, or sports, success after college requires teamwork skills.

**Rugby, for those who play, polishes that "team facet" on the jewel that is a college experience.**

Jimmy Parker took on the role of coaching those we needed developed at USD. Jimmy has a wonderful knack for having those mostly newer players recognize that they were with Jimmy because there was an urgency to get them ready to start. Their practices were designed to give them the basic skills, insights and repetitions to be able to contribute when given the nod. In American college rugby that development needs to be in weeks, not years.

An illustration of what we had at SDSU: When we were organizing a reunion for the 20th anniversary of our National Championship, everyone on the roster was invited and almost everyone came. Jimmy recalls a memorable moment: A player thanked an organizer for having been included, even though they'd been a perennial third stringer and so not really part of the championship team. Warren Stanley, superstar flanker on the starting side overheard and commented, "You were on my team."

# TO RUCK OR TO MAUL IN THE COLLEGE GAME

It is the case that there is very little practice time for college teams.  These players are first students, then players. Decisions must be made by coaches about what to teach and what there is just not time to teach.  During a rugby game, the ball does go to the ground.  There has never been an exception: In every rugby game, ball on the ground must be managed.  Therefore, if how to deal with ball on the ground must be taught, let's just put ball at a breakdown on the ground every time.  Let's ruck.  Further, right now it is pretty much accepted that comparing rucked ball (ball on the ground) to mauled ball (ball in hand) rucked ball is generally faster.  Faster ball sometimes means relaunching an attack before the defense is ready. Oooo, that is nice. So, as a team skill to teach, spend that practice time teaching the team to ruck.

Another little thing: It takes two to form a ruck, three for a maul. Let's save that extra player to do something besides bind to a teammate.

One part of the game at which mauling can be an almost essential tactic is at lineout, particularly down near their goal line. That skill can be taught later in the season, to just the forwards. You can play an entire game without mauling. In every single game, ball on the ground must be rucked.

In 1969 at UCLA we generally mauled. When caught in possession or approached by a would-be tackler we turned, presenting the ball to arriving support. If the ball was on the ground, our first and best option was to pick it up. My, we were primitive! My, we won a lot! Agreed to team tactics win games.

The game changed from breakdowns being seen as failures to multiphase styles with breakdowns often scripted. Still the Greenwood principles of "Go Forward, Support, Continuity and Pressure" still provide valuable structure with which to evaluate play.

# MOST BASIC THINGS AND ENCOURAGING QUESTIONS

One day it was raining hard, and we could not use our natural turf field. We were in a classroom having a chalk talk or skull session. At some point, it became clear that one player, who was new to the game, was unfamiliar with the term "find touch". I then made a mistake: I asked a returning All-American, an important team leader, to help. The look on his face — yikes, he didn't know either! I blurted out a correct answer and asked if he agreed. We pretty much dodged embarrassment, but it was close.

Later, the All American and I talked about it. During his age-group rugby career, he explained that he had always been the star. He thought he was expected to know many things, some of which he did not, but at that point, he felt he couldn't ask as he was the star. He had been stuck for many years.

Interestingly, the concept of touch will not be familiar to those transitioning to rugby from American football, where it is referred to as as out of bounds.

Some may not be aware that the lines marking the edges of the field of play, known as "sidelines," are out of bounds or "in touch." To "find touch" means to have a kicked ball land on or beyond the line or be touched by a player who is on or beyond the line. The width of the marked line can be up to 12 centimeters or 5 inches.

Note: In the official "Laws of the Game," there are 334 references to touch. Most of what defines finding touch is in Law 18. The information is too extensive to include here, but it is not too much to be understood particularly by wings and fullbacks who need to know their options.

# PASS THE BALL STRAIGHT ACROSS THE FIELD

Hyperbole: I believe this is the most important team principle ever taught. My disappointment was immense when I watched the All Blacks fail to win the World Cup. Their ball in attack was not flat and, in my self-righteous, all-the-valor-of-the-non-combatant, and pompous opinion, cost them the championship.

Note: This is NOT a best practice in 7's. This does not apply to passes from the scrumhalf to the kicker in tactical kicking situations.

That said, here is our discussion:

In rugby, players have the freedom to pass the ball in any direction, as long as it does not travel towards the opponent's goal line. The ball carrier may adjust the direction of the pass according to the receiver›s position. This can be very difficult, as the ball carrier, burdened by carrying the ball and being the target of tacklers, must assess, before making a pass, too many things: The depth, direction of the run, distance, pace, and readiness of the potential receiver. Furthermore, the receiver cannot anticipate the direction of the incoming pass and must be prepared for anything, causing hesitancy and uncertainty. Also, if catching the ball other than even with the ball carrier, the receiver must go further to reach the gain line.

Better option: Pass the ball straight across the field. It then becomes the responsibility of the receiver to take a position of depth, enabling them to accelerate forward when the ball is approaching. They should extend both hands towards the ball carrier, aiming to touch the ball first with the far hand, ideally at chest height. This position allows them to see the ball, the field ahead, defenders, and with that information assess available options. The receiver has been calling out the name of the ball carrier with a confident and encouraging tone.

The ball carrier is running straight up the field and has an idea of where his teammate is because they are hearing their name. The ball carrier will ALWAYS look before passing. Since the ball will be delivered straight across the field, the ball carrier need only turn the head, without turning their shoulders.

There is no occasion in rugby for the no-look pass. (It might be important in basketball and perhaps team handball, but not here.) Indeed, looking—turning one's head, can be an element of very effective dummies.

When ready, the ball carrier delivers the ball so that it does not travel towards the opponents' goal. Thus both the passer and receiver, and EVERYBODY on the team knows precisely where the ball and the receiver are and will be. This is a significant team advantage.

When practiced, this option can improve a bad tendency to run diagonally across the field. Imagine, please, no more reaching behind for the errant ball, no balls knocked-on because of passing miscues, all balls taken at pace with support ready for the next link. It has worked for us.

This team skill must be practiced. At most practice sessions, we use drills organized in grids and columns. This skill is mostly practiced in columns. The principle of receiving the ball at pace, level with the passer, enables the receiver to have all the options that the original ball carrier had moments before, providing an advantageous way to play.

Working the principles with passing lines of 5, trying it while standing still, or pantomiming without balls, and/or shouting "burst" as the receiver anticipates the ball, emphasizing that the ball should reach the center of the end of the middle finger of the far hand before reaching the receiver's body, all these details collectively contribute to building a stronger team.

# NEAR TOUCH, USE THE OUTSIDE SHOULDER

When the ball carrier runs near the touchline, the ball carrier should engage any opponent with the outside shoulder.

- Prevents being bundled into touch, and it would be their put-in for the lineout.
- Allows the ball carrier to assess support, as when they use their outside shoulder to engage the tackler they have all their options, including maybe a pop-pass to that bursting support. Wouldn't that be nice?

# NO BAD PASSES

This is a commitment to one another. All have accepted that possession in rugby is crucial; there is really nothing more important. Can't score without it. Possession can be lost for various reasons, many of which are beyond one's control. Working on passing and working on passing and working on passing and working on passing can minimize the chances of losing possession during the game. When tempted to make an awkward, risky pass, DON'T. Go into an opponent, go to touch, just get low and stable, but no bad passes.

It becomes a judgment, and yes, some players can execute passes that others cannot, especially when connecting with a predictable teammate, one with whom they have drilled in practice. Come game time, as a coach, all you can do is silently second guess from touch.

# TUCK YOUR EARS

Safety and the prevention of catastrophic injuries - this concept of tucking your ears is the same as shrugging your shoulders. It is the opposite of sticking your neck out. It reduces the likelihood of the neck being forced into a harmful position. It should be done at tackles, when entering loose play, and during engagement of set scrums. This point is typically emphasized to players just entering their rugby experience. Comes naturally to most.

When teaching tackling and walking through concepts such as keeping the head behind, some new players tend to drop their shoulders, almost as if they are reaching with their head. They should not do this. Tucking the ears brings the entire body closer to the ball carrier, possibly with one knee in front. That is good.

Another point on tackling: Full-speed tackling drills have resulted in more players being unavailable due to injury than any other part of training. While repetitions are a part of learning, full-speed tackling drills are not worth the risk. Players can become proficient and learn safe techniques at a walking pace and off-pace, with very little full-speed drills or full-go scrimmaging.

# BEND YOUR KNEES

Seems so simple, but humans have options. When we want to bring our hands closer to the ground, we can either bend at the waist or bend our knees. (We can also fall down, but we are taking that off the table.) In rugby, there is generally an advantage to having a lower center of gravity. Our center of gravity when standing is located approximately halfway between the front and back, an inch below the belly button. When we bend at the waist, we are primarily bending at the hips, which are just slightly below the center of gravity. When we bend at the waist to lower our upper body and hands, our center of gravity remains unchanged, (actually it moves forward, but does not change much in terms of height).

We want our center of gravity lower because we are more stable, with increased resistance to being knocked over, and we are better set mechanically to take an opponent off their feet. When we bend our knees to get low, we can also see much better because our upper body and head are closer to upright.

So, when you want to pick up a ball from the ground or support a teammate who has just gone down with the ball, or go into a tackle, … bend your knees. For tall players, the only time your height is an advantage is when you are going up for a ball. To get down where the rest of the game is being played, bend your knees.

# RUN STRAIGHT UP FIELD

This is almost the same as passing the ball straight across the field. We want to be able to support one another. Support is much easier if we know where the ball carrier is headed. The laws allow the ball carrier to run in any direction.

There is only one direction in which the goal line, and scoring points, are found. Let's just all agree to go in that direction.

Player: "But coach, the evil people that want to tackle me are that way."

Coach to player: "You know how to get low and go into them, knocking them off their feet and thus disfiguring the defense, right?

Player: "Yes, coach."

Coach: "And if you do that, your teammates will enjoy supporting you, right? "

Player: "Yes, coach."

Coach: "And your choice to try to outflank them by running at an angle across the field will make it more difficult for your forwards to get to the breakdown, and they will hate you, right?"

Player: "Yes, coach."

Coach: "And wouldn't it be nice to produce beautiful, quick "juice" ball with which your team can score?"

Player: "Yes, coach."

Coach: "So, if you can't just do a little side step or swerve and continue straight up the field, you should follow our team plan and create a solid ruck instead of trying to show off."

Player: "Ok, coach."

# UNIFY THE CONSTRUCT

One of the reasons for my poor hearing is that I stood in the wrong place while running a drill used to unify the construct of our pack. Most packs will agree that to execute a well-coordinated shove in the set, they should be capable of at least counting in unison. Seems obvious, right?

As a drill, our pack, or even more than eight forwards at a time, would form a circle, facing inwards, bound to one another, reaching around, hand to shoulder. I would instruct them to squeeze, then sink, and then jump in unison into the air, shouting "Ya!" This was to be on my count of "2, 3, Ya." I would position myself in the center and provide a deliberate cadence, "2, 3," expecting the interval between the 2 and the 3 to match the the interval between the 3 and the Ya! The result, early in the season or with a new pack, was horrible. Their timing was terribly off, resulting in shoulders being painfully yanked and heads bumped. The

"Ya's" were spread out over what seemed like several seconds. All involved immediately realized that tighter binds, with not only shoulders but hips held tightly together, were needed. They also focused on the interval between the 2 and the 3. When they got it right, the "Ya!" was literally deafening, and the jump into the air was high, coordinated, and pain free.

This drill illustrated to those involved that the forces generated in a united shove were far stronger than the sum of any eight individuals. (Although this is probably even better demonstrated on the scrum machine.) The concept applies to binding in the maul, if your team mauls.

I now have the scrumhalf stand in the middle. (Joking. Stand outside the circle.)

# EXPLODE THE TACKLE

Some runners, especially those with a good sidestep or stutter move, will receive a ball at pace. Then, when faced with a potential tackler, they almost halt their forward progress in an attempt to deceive the tackler into falling for their side-step-stutter-step dance routine. This is a common issue that should be explained in a one-on-one conversation with the runner.

An example was a wing for San Diego State, Bruce Markey. He may have been the most athletic runner on the team, easily standing at 6'2" and weighing 210 pounds with a 32-inch waist. When he would do something like a 6-in, a play where he would receive the ball just to the side of the set piece, often with a single defender in front of him, he would typically perform his fancy footwork, and get by. In a game against a better opponent he tried that move, only to be tackled by the defender. He was frustrated as at lower levels this had not been a problem. During the half time break, we discussed the concept that a bullet can kill an elk because the kinetic energy of the fast-moving bullet was dissipated into the tissues of the elk. It was exploding!

Early in the second half, another 6-in was called. That poor defender had no idea of time, place, or who did it. Bruce had just run through the guy, and almost lost his balance as he got to the far side. I almost felt guilty.

# NEVER PUNCH THE GROUND

This is another coaching style comment. It is very common to see a player make a mistake – dropping a pass is a common incentive, then drop to their knees, punching the ground, and declaring to the world, "My fault!" They then proceeded to stomp in a little circle, engaging in a sort of self-flagellation dance. This should not ever happen!

It is effective for a coach, at the very next opportunity, to privately converse with that player:

- Remind the player of the incident. They had been hard on themselves. Then explain:
- Everybody already knows that you screwed up, so you need not "own up."
- Drawing attention to our team's mistake does nothing positive
- While you were doing that, you could have been getting to your blocks for the next play, thus being part of a disciplined team.

- We need you

Avoid criticizing the behavior in public. Do it face-to-face, one-on-one, privately.
    Works every time.

## SKILLS AT PACE

Ron Mayes once said something to the effect of: "Teach them skills, skills at pace, then let them play."

To this, I would humbly add, to the list of things to teach, skills when knackered. This dovetails with another concept discussed later in this book, practice with perfection, so that when pace and fatigue make perfection unattainable, you will still be good enough to win.

# GET TO YOUR BLOCKS

Blocks here are starting blocks. A team should launch an attack or defense after aligning with each other and being aware of the offside line and the opposition. The back line players in first phase attack should be positioned in a stance that deters players from moving at an angle away from the ball. To achieve this, backs should have their outside foot forward, arms should be reaching to the inside, and players should be turned to show the number on their back to the teammate outside them. This disciplined stance is not only effective in preventing bad running angles, but it looks good and can make the opponent respect what they are seeing.

The angle of the backline should be such that if the ball were launched straight across the field, and each back in succession kept passing the ball wide, successive players sprinting straight up the field could just catch the ball. This would often position the starting blocks in a line from the flyhalf, extending at an angle greater than 45 degrees. As a team aligns deeper in their own territory, the angle of the backline starting blocks should never be deeper than the goal line corner flag, so we get shallower as we get deeper into the defensive end of the field.

Spacing, which refers to how far out on the line the players set up, is often determined by weather conditions, the width of the pitch, and of course, the location of the mark. Both angle and spacing can be tweaked based on insights gained from unopposed backline handling drills during practice.

In defense, the feet are positioned behind the line, enabling the defender to have their chest over the offside line. Spacing is based on the position of the opponent being marked. This is beyond the scope of this booklet. The lesson here is that you should reach the starting blocks as soon as possible, with your body position confirming your competence.

# PLAY ON THE BOIL

Barry Legh, at UBC, was overheard saying, "We are off the boil now." The implication was that he was wondering how he might get his team back to the team intensity he called "the boil." We discussed this later, at the post-game. He had no easy answers, but it does warrant thought.

It is my belief that there is nothing that a coach or player can say to a team that will bring them to the desired level of arousal, playing "...on the boil."

I remember arriving at a Tucson Tournament long ago and seeing my team ahead of me, gathering at our field. One member raised his hands and shouted, "We are here to win." That declaration might have been caused by the fact that in the prior few visits this team did not reasonably have winning on their radar. This trip might be different. I thought to myself, how uninspiring that was. I guess a few of his mates may have had it dawn on them, "Gosh, maybe he's right." I wish that player had just played very intensely.

When I had the opportunity to speak at the induction of Chris Lippert, OMBAC, Eagle, Barbarian, into the USA Rugby Hall of Fame, I contacted some of his former teammates for research on what I should say. "Chris's strength came with few words and direct results." When I spoke with Stevie Marshall, the tight head in the front row of the 1987 team, his first recollection was: "… during an early season game" he recalled Chris, "… running by me and whispering, "We got this," " a phrase frequently used by Chris and teammates throughout that year. Leadership by example as a teammate.

The front row in rugby is unique in sport. - The athletes are in physical contact, battling, when the ball is not in play. One opponent, who wished to remain anonymous, recalled being taken to the sky lab by Chris and characterized his style as "sincere."

Summary Statement: No clichés. Inspire by playing up, by example, not by shouting "let's go!" (despite Tom Brady's tendency to do just that). Lift your teammates by being the one to step up. If everyone on a team steps up, things boil.

# CHIN OFF YOUR CHEST

At first glance this might seem to be a safety element, like, "Tuck your ears," and to some extent it is, the main intent of this chin-off-your-chest technique is, half-jokingly, to deceive the referee.

It is not legal to enter a ruck and intentionally fall on the far side of the ball or onto the ball carrier on the ground. Simply keeping the chin off the chest is another way to just have your head slightly raised. This allows you to see, no matter how low you are, and it makes it appear that you are positively contributing to a successful ruck. We would typically coach arriving forwards to get low enough so that they could place their forearms on the player who took the ball in. This can appear as if they are going over to illegally seal possession. With their chin lifted off the chest, it does not appear that their intention is to go down on the far side. Hopefully, the referee will see them as trying to be positive and produce clean ball.

## TWO HANDS ON THE BALL

This is not exactly our rule, although it is generally accepted as sound advice. - Instead, our rule is that a ball carrier should have at least two points of contact with the ball. Each hand and the chest all count as potential points of contact. What is not okay is holding the ball in one hand away from the body. It is okay to curl the ball in one arm so that the ball also touches the chest. Indeed, this option allows the other hand to fend off a tackler with the other hand (straight arm). This option also allows the free hand and arm to cushion or control the descent to the ground for a try.

If you are gifted such that when you grasp the ball you can touch your long finger to your thumb, this rule does not apply to you.

# DIVE OUT OF THE POOL

Bing Dawson's legendary OMBAC teams embraced this concept. Everybody knows how to dive into a pool, but when one contemplates standing in the shallow end and trying to jump out – that is the notion of going from low to high in a tackle, exploding low to high. It helps some people improve mechanics, especially when it comes to tackling and clearing opponents from the loose.

# DOUBLE BOUNCE TRY

Kevin Higgins, Eagle and world class outside center, fullback and winger, scored a lot! He often crossed the goal line unmolested. He would then fall forward, with the ball on his chest, bouncing twice in the process, the "double bounce try."

    A couple of decades later, the Navy Women made a t-shirt with "Double Bounce Try," printed on the front. Go figure.

# SHOW GLEE AFTER TRIES

This is a lesson that Del Chipman, superlative Eagle winger, learned the hard way. Del was someone who scored a lot. It became so common that sometimes he would score and then, quite nonchalantly, start jogging back for the ensuing kickoff. One time the ref's view was obscured. That ref saw Del Chipman's nonchalance and figured he had not scored and did not award the try. From that event forward, Del jumped and waved hands in celebration, whether he had scored or not.

# KICK TO OURSELVES OR TO TOUCH

Touch, Box,
Up and Under/Garryowen,
Grubber, Wiper

Those are five basic tactical kicks. For college level play we should NEVER kick away possession of the ball. Jimmy Parker prefers: Kicking should improve position or possession. I prefer Jimmy's positive wording but would never admit it.

**Touch**: If kicking to the near touch line, find touch or make it short enough that your teammate could catch the ball.

**Box**: If kicking high trying for that area just behind your own pack, "the box," make the kick short enough that your forwards can get there. If the opponent catches it, no matter how many of your forwards are there, if the opposition is any good they will win the loose even if all of your forwards arrive after the fact.

**Up and Under**: The high deep up-an-under is to be avoided. The exception: If your teammate can actually get there and compete for the ball. Note: sometimes they might seem to work early in the game, but later it becomes a big factor that the deep opposition must run far shorter distances to get under the ball than your on-side teammates. That said, if in trouble later in the game and desperate, it can be tried, as it did work for Garryowen. (The Club in Limerick, not the Irish jig or password for US 1st Calvary.) Just ask Chris O'Brien, arguably the best Eagle kicker ever, who spent all night kicking to the Argentinian fullback an April 7, 1990, with zero positive effect. (My assessment)

**Grubber**: Good grubbers are wonderful. They must be practiced. They are taken from a gap in the defense – arguably if you can safely grubber then you could have run it – but that is less fun if the defender is going to be jumping on your back. Good to know: That ball that is rolling seemingly randomly is going to, every time, bounce up. When it bounces up its pace forward goes way down. So, if you have moved to be chasing it from directly behind, it will bounce up into your hands, and the crowd goes wild.

**Wiper**: Kicks to far touch, the wiper, must either find touch or be caught by teammates. If the opponent gets it, likely they will do something that is to their advantage.

For college level teams, especially ones with better kickers – kicks should find touch or be fielded by the kicking team. That is a period at the end of sentence, for emphasis! Kick to ourselves or find touch!

## CALL FOR THE BALL

When OMBAC and Eagle lock Bill Leversee called out, "Chief's ball!" several truisms flashed.

- This was Chief's ball. No doubt about it.
- Teammates could assume their roles at a Chief's ball
- The opposition tilted their heads in wonder at the confidence communicated by Chief's tone and, deep inside, wanted no part of it.

A player who judges that a high ball is theirs should immediately, loudly, and with an unambiguous tone announce their intent to the whole world. In addition to the effects listed under Chief's ball above, the opposition will develop a sense that they are playing against a team with a consistent, disciplined, and unifying plan. To the extent that a team can demotivate an opponent, they should. (Within the constraints of fair play).

Our player who has called for the ball must then follow through. Very rarely, a misjudgment will become clear. Only the player who called for the ball can call it off. If they have heard or otherwise discovered a teammate who is clearly in a better position, a loud declaration, using the new players name, can be done. The new player then screams with enthusiasm their commitment to that ball. Usually this would take just too much time. The original caller must be the receiver.

For high balls that are coming down to a crowd, our catcher must get there and turn side on, so as not to knock on if the catch is missed. First support assumes a position of protection, close buy and sometimes even able to lift the receiver.

When the catcher is not pressured, first support quickly gets way back. It is amazing how long it takes to catch a ball and then get it into your hands and assess your options that might include popping to support. It is difficult to get too deep.

I remember a Cal left wing taking a high ball we had kicked. One of Cal's cadre of fast, hard and straight running backs, coming from what must have been 20 yards back, took a pop pass at full pace. I thought we were in for a long night. (We were, but we won, on our way to a national championship). I knew I wanted teams I coached to do what I had just seen, a wing standing still giving the ball to a fast super-athlete coming at full pace.

# NEVER LET THE HIGH BALL BOUNCE

There are times when a receiver just cannot get there for the high ball, or it is going to be close. The receiver might be tempted to stop running to the ball and let it bounce. DON'T!

- The opposition can't see the situation as well as you can, so they must continue to zero in on you, thus keeping them out of optimally defending what develops.
- You might get there or make a shoestring recovery. (Remember to turn to lower risk of knocking on.)
- How a rugby ball will bounce defies analysis with the highest math extant. Can't be done. Don't try.
- Your teammates are running to deep support, so they will be in better positions to deal with the ball that you miss than will you.

# BETTER LATE

A repeated concept in this game is that low and fast, arriving on the burst, is desirable. That is why we ask our players to set up so far back in all phases of attack. Further, arriving early is not just a benign mistiming. Arriving early has the potential to put you offsides, be in the way of a better attacker, or just not be able to contribute positively. So, better to be there low, hard and a little late than early, with nothing good to do.

## PRACTICE WITH PERFECTION

This especially goes for experienced players. In almost every college program athletes new to the game will soon be starting. If every player wants every player to contribute maximally it is incumbent on the best players to provide examples. Nothing is beneath anyone. For better, more experienced players, this can require self-discipline when doing such things as simple passing lines at walk pace. However, the best players, from whom new players can learn the most, will be:

- Getting in proper starting block position
- Calling teammate by name
- Paying attention, focused, always
- Reaching for the ball
- Taking the ball out of the air before it gets to their body, far hand touching first
- Passing it on in a single step

- Passing the ball perfectly straight across the field, dead ball with axis up and down if less than 3 yards, spin with leading end just higher than the tail if more than three yards
- Immediately after the pass moving into deep support

The experienced players should be demonstrating how they would like these newcomers to eventually play. Practice with attention to detail, with perfection, so if, in the pressure and fatigue of a game, you aren't perfect, you are still good enough to win.

## DON'T LOSE THE F BALL

This is not here because one would ever say it. It is here as a reminder that we don't want our teammates to ever have to think that phrase when giving you possession. Don't be that guy who loses possession of the ball. Rather, do all the things one does to protect possession: Low center of gravity; wide base of support; bend your knees; two hands on the ball; explode the tackle; yada, yada, yada. Each time you handle the ball you don't need to score or set up a teammate for the 60 yd gallop. Just don't lose possession. Don't lose the Ball.

# NOT JUST "WITH YOU"

Let your teammate know you are in support, with your teammate's NAME, not just "with you". The tone we seek is "Hello ball, hello friend," as championed by Bill Freeman, New Zealand Director of Coaching, on his coaching clinic tour to LA so long ago. Even better than just telling your ballcarrier teammate you are there, using your mate's name tells the opposition that you are part of a team of friends. Admittedly a little thing, but little things can add up to make a real difference.

# SLACKEN, SHORTEN, STRAIGHTEN, SWERVE/SHOOT, SPRINT

These are the five S's of a successful sidestep or swerve move. Ball carrier slows down/**s**lackens, so as to make the physics of change of direction easier. **S**horter stride length is further enabling changing direction to run **s**traight at the defender, requiring the defender to square up to the attacker's direction. The ball carrier can then begin an s-shaped **s**werve, causing the defender to leave his squared position only to discover to late that the ball carrier has resumed a straight up the field line and started to sprint.

Alternatively, the ball carrier, having slowed shortened stride and straightened to be running directly at the defender, then shoots to one side and sprints to freedom.

The difference between the swerve and the sidestep is that in the swerve the s-shaped running starts early such that the defender must move from the squared-up position. With the sidestep, the final move is later, just before it would be too late, and the tackler could get you, a sharp singular shoot, typically to the original line of attack, leaves the defender frozen still. Both the swerve and the sidestep end with a **s**print.

# JUICE BALL TO THE WING

What's juice ball? – that is the ball that appears very quickly, sitting still, at the back foot of the loose, before the defense can get themselves set. Our scrumhalf, and 11 or 12 teammates are in their starting blocks, drooling. They have to wipe the juice from their lips before launching the next phase. Juice ball is really fun!

Of course, sometimes it takes longer than would be ideal for the ball to be available. Such delays do allow the defensive backs to prepare and therefore a successful outside strike is less likely to succeed. NOTE, since we have not committed more that 2 or rarely 3 forwards to the loose, our remaining forwards have positioned themselves well back, even 7 to 10 yards back. As that ball comes slowly available, they burst forward such that a simple straight up and down pop pass comes to the hands of the lead forward runner. Only then can the defense leave their side of the offside line – at the back foot of that loose. So, our big gnarly strong ball carrier is coming at full force, ball on chest, with a couple of mates right behind, while the defender is just rolling onto their toes. What's not to like?

Oh, and if the scrumhalf decides not to give the gnarly friend the ball, the defense still must respect our threatened redrive. This kind of thing soon gets old for the defense.

There is a fine line, not fully defined by the referees, between slowing down after not getting the ball, and obstruction.

If it was quick juice ball, the deeply positioned forwards are optimally set to support the wider attack, which will be spun in front of them.

Summarizing: Slow ball can go to redriving forwards. Quick ball to the wing!

# BALL'S OUT!

It is the case at every line out, set piece or loose that not everyone can see the ball. Often it is the player in the role of scrumhalf and only one or two others who know when the ball is to be put into play. It behooves a team to know when that ball is out. Obvious as that sounds, it is worth mentioning that the instant a team knows it is out they can launch the defense or attack, in unison. If the ref is not sure of the timing, the ref is compelled to think that the whole side can't be wrong. Further, launching together helps maintain back line spacing. Launching together looks disciplined, like that side has it together.

Therefore, it has become our practice for anyone and everyone who can see the ball about to be launched to emphatically declare, "Balls out!"

# LAMA LAMA!

Old Mission Beach Athletic Club or OMBAC fields a rugby program. They were the perennial National Champions for about a decade. They had some wonderful, colorful players. Among those players were some pacific islanders including Sammy Vaca, Solo Komai, and Harold McFayden. There were moves by the islanders that were very special, enjoyable to see and imitate. Those athletes had flare. At OMBAC that flare came to be, "Lama Lama!"

Good rugby teams do things with a little "Lama Lama!

## YOU GOTTA BUY THE T-SHIRT

- Yes, in college rugby you even must pay for it, but that is not what we are trying to explain here
- Buying the t-shirt means declaring commitment to what you are about
- It means that there will be no "if only" –No withhold - -no reserve, nothing held back to use as an excuse.  This T-shirt is something with which I label myself
- It means testing the rugby gods, by printing the Championship Ts before the final game. (Been there, did that, loved it.)
- It means wearing a T-shirt, with any one or all of that litany of options to which so much of this pamphlet is dedicated, and finding it cool to know what they mean

Now understand, there is a risk.  If you buy the t-shirt, and you **lose**, it is going to hurt, and hurt worse. But, the risk of that failure is lower, and, even losing on the scoreboard, you and your teammates **have the satisfaction of best efforts shared.**

# SURVIVOR TO PLAYER

Please, all of you who have played, think back to the first time you were caught in possession. It was probably at practice but could have been a game. You were immediately swarmed, aggressively, dangerously. It was awful. Reflexively you protected genitals and face. Then the threat disappeared. The ball had disappeared as well. Who cared? Why am I here? That was you, the **survivor**. Then you got better at the game.

The vignette I'm about to share is how we did it a couple of decades ago. People and rugby do change. So, if you are thinking, "That's not right," you're probably right.

Eventually, you again became the ball carrier.

This time you had positioned yourself well back from a teammate with the ball. You shouted your teammate's name, with a conspiring tone of: "Hello, friend."

Your teammate with the ball looks then passes, straight across field, chest high. You had to burst. You touch it first with the far hand, before it reaches your body, immediately securing it with the other. "Hello ball."

You can see the ball and the field in one view.

Despite your teammate having drawn their defender, it is clear that you will not be breaking with this one. You choose an opponent and straighten your run, keeping that opponent between you and their goal line.

Boom! You expend your kinetic energy, like a bullet kills a boar, going low to high, as if diving out of a pool, into your nemesis' chest.

The would-be tackler is surprised as they are now unweighted and being pushed back. Another opponent must enter the fray to slow your progress. You have thus further disfigured their defense.

You then **violently** take yourself down, upper body oriented east-west, leaving the defenders on their feet. Those opponents are wondering what is happening just as your teammates blow over you, clearing them like debris.

Now you place quick, clear, controlled "juice" ball, arm's length, straight back from your belly button. Your scrumhalf is right there, wiping the drool from smiling lips before the ball is gleefully launched to the next phase.

All that can see scream, "Balls Out!"

You feel good about it.

You're up, eagerly off to the next chance.

Alas, no next break down, as the quick ball to the wing resulted in a double bounce try.

 You are now a **player**.

So, rugby is a crucible for the process of learning to help. It attracts and develops good, helpful, fun people. People like you.

# STACK MEMORY

When working, for instance, with passing lines early in the season, almost any observer will see many, many, many things that need work, even after just the first run-through. From the basic mechanics of how the drills work to what a player is doing while awaiting their next go, spin versus dead ball and ... the coaching points are innumerable. One could spend an entire practice segment reciting a litany of little things we'd all like to be done just right. Obviously, that would not be of value, because humans, especially humans who are trying to perform complex skills, just cannot deal with such a tall stack of skills.

In the early 1990's there were handheld calculators that used reverse polish logic and stack memory. That kind of memory was such that when too many items were loaded, the earlier loaded items began to fall off the stack, and were lost. Such are the minds of players.

As a coach it is difficult to limit yourself, but your players can process only a very limited stack of items that need focus in whatever time segment, e.g., a couple of 35 yard passing lines.  There is some pretty good research that suggests that three succinct points at each intervention may be optimal. Look then pass, burst onto the ball, and reach for the ball, would be an ambitious three items.  Sometimes it is best to let the lines run through a few reps before adding more suggestions.  Keep in mind that what you are really doing as a coach is adding additional points to those you have already made. You are making those points to winded kids experiencing something close to sensory overload already. It is so tempting to spue your limitless knowledge.  Don't.

# COACHES IN CAHOOTS AND HALFTIME HOUSEKEEPING

Halftime of a game is 15 minutes or less. In tournament play with shortened halves it can be just 7 to 10 minutes. Hydration, attention to injuries, and rest are all needed. It might be typical in your program to have **five** types of communication: **One on one** – a coach to a single player, to encourage a single behavior; **forwards coach** to the pack, making at most three points; **backs coach to the backline**, with same max of three points; **captain to the team**, at most two points. The captain can recognize another player who wishes to speak. The forwards and back pieces can be done simultaneously. (Typically, our scrumhalf would be with the forwards for this.) So where is the head coach? The head coach gathered the other coaches a few minutes before half and they come to agreement on who is going to cover what. Coming to that agreement starts by eliciting suggestions. There is a fine line between planning what is going to happen at half and being dogmatic, so the head coach needs take care.

The group of coaches must know that this pre-halftime get together is going to happen. The trainer needs to bring what is needed to the player, and not take the player from the group. The head coach must see to all of this.

As the team gets some experience, they will come to know what is going to happen at halftime. Before the ref is calling to restart, the players, without coaches, should have their coordinated hands-in vocal, be it "2,3 **ya!**", or "1,2,3 **USD**", 1,2,3 **Go Navy**, or whatever. Looking here for a sense of all in, not necessarily volume or perfect unison. Each to their own. This would be timed such that the players are not rushed taking the field – perhaps sending the message to the opposition that we are ready and eager to resume play.

# ECCLESIASTES 9:10

*Whatsoever thy hand findeth to do, do it with thy might.* That's the first part of Ecclesiastes 9:10, from the Old Testament. The "t" of the "thy" is lowercase – God is there, but **you** must do it.

This is the only quote from the Bible in this manifesto. No further explanation required.

# CLASS ACT

I remember so well bringing USD to play Loyola in Baltimore, Maryland, where I started coaching in 1979. Loyola's side was captained by Sean Lugano. What a privilege to play against Sean. We use him here to illustrate the concept of "class act." He was killed in 911.

The game went well for both sides. We were fortunate to score more points. I remember the game certainly not because USD scored more points – rather, for me, three things:

- We made Juice Ball.
- Something that happened right after the match, and
- A comment made at the after-match Mentioned under the topic of college players wanting to know "Why?" (So not repeated here.)

Our forwards, at USD, were not paid to run with flare or to pass. Starting from depth, they drove straight up field, blew low to high into one or more defenders, took it down, body east-west, and put the ball back, belly level, arm's length. 1 or 2, rarely 3 other forwards blew over the top, spines in lines to the far side of that ball. They made juice ball. Juice ball to the wing, so more of our backs got to do their gazelle imitations, striding, perhaps with some moves just for show, a little "Lama Lama," to dive down in goal, bouncing twice, hair un-mussed. We got more juice ball, therefore we won. Our entire team felt good about having bought into this game plan.

Have you ever tried to put words to what it is to be a "class act?" For me, it is that special quality in a person with whom I'd like to spend more time, to get to know. Selfishly, spending time with them would make me better. They are the type of person with whom one wants to share not just a beer but a meal. Right after the Loyola game, Sean Lugano, with no fanfare, but with eye contact and a sincere handshake, thanked me for the game. Just recently I was recounting this experience to a wonderful player and gentleman, Kevin Barrett, a USD Hall of Famer, who I had forgotten was the fullback in that game. He interrupted me to say, "I remember that guy, the halfback who thanked us. Class act, that man."

# SPIDERMAN

In the Spiderman movie, *No way Home*, Aunt May dies. Late in the show there is a scene at her grave. I missed the dialog, but was taken by the epitaph etched on her tombstone, which was: "If you **help someone**, you **help everyone**." That's Rugby! **Rugby is helping and being helped.** One could say that learning this game is about the **process** of becoming helpful.

# REMEMBERING

I remember only one of the final scores of the hundreds of games in which I've been involved.  That score was 10-9.  It is remembered not because it was a national championship, but because Air Force momentarily lost focus, allowing us to quick tap for the score.  Glaring take-home lesson: Just as one can get better at skills like passing and tackling, one can get better at paying attention.  I remember that score because that game could be used as **a parable on the process of getting better at the skill of paying attention**.

It behooves the team seeking improvement to expect one another to pay attention, stay focused, during the entirety of every practice, so it will be your norm in every game.

# DR. ARNOLD BEISSER

Another reason I do not remember scores is because of something from Dr. Arnold Beisser, a polio victim, quadriplegic and largely respirator dependent member of the psychiatry faculty at UCLA.

I came across an article about this man when I stopped for breakfast near LAX, having just dropped off two California Grizzley candidates from a trial we had attended at UCLA. The *LA Times* newspaper was dated April 8, 1990, and the byline was ARNOLD R. BEISSER. (Yet it was written mostly in the third person – go figure.)

Part of the article read:

> At 24, Arnold R. Beisser, having graduated from Stanford Medical School, completed his internship and planned for a surgical residency. But it was 1950, the United States was fighting in Korea, and

> *Beisser, a Naval reservist, was alerted that he was to be called to active duty. His residency had to be put on hold.*
>
> *In the four months before his orders came, he devoted himself to his second love, tennis, winning a national championship and a high national ranking. He was young, strong, healthy and seemingly invincible. Then, a few days after his 25th birthday, he was stricken with polio, paralyzed from the neck down. For two years, he would live in an iron lung, and any further recovery was minimal.*

In Dr. Beisser's book, *Flying without Wings*, I was struck with the inherent validity and weight of the following: Asked what it was like to be continuously so perilously close to death, he responded: **Life is often treated like a competitive sport, as though dying were the equivalent of losing. That is unfortunate because it dooms us all to be losers eventually. If the focus is only on the outcome of something, one misses the process.**

The amalgamated processes of life are woven into our game of Rugby. Winning is nice. The process of learning to win and learning to be humble when you do, those are even better. Dr. Beisser said it more elegantly:

*A person can learn much from defeat ... forbearance and discipline, the ability to endure and to take the bitter with the sweet, as well as what must be done to win the next time.*

## FINAL THOUGHT

There was a time, while I was doing it, that I wondered about the prudence of allowing Rugby to be such a big part of my life. Predicating my happiness on the behavior of sometimes intoxicated college age kids. Now, with quite a different point of view. I don't wonder any more. I am totally OK with having coached.

Choose your team approach, do it with might, in rugby and life.

# WILLIAM LAUGHLIN VETTER, M.D., FACS RUGBY RESUME

BS, Physical Education, 1973, UCLA
MS, Kinesiology, 1975, UCLA
MD, 1978, UCLA
Internship and residency, Johns Hopkins Hospital, Baltimore, Maryland
Board Certified, Orthopedic Surgery
Fellowship trained in Sports Medicine/Arthroscopy and in Hand Surgery
Started rugby1969 at UCLA, with Coach Dennis Storer
Started coaching at Loyola University, Maryland, 1979. (Kenny Ames' fault)
Simultaneously helped to start and coached Baltimore County RFC (BACON), EPRU
Made a careful effort to enrich his rugby and coaching with:

- Took all three levels of USAFU Coaching, (in the 80's)
- All three levels of the RIU program, with Jim Greenwood, from Loughborough
- Toured with the Junior Eagles, as the doc and listener
- Coached the Southern California Collegiates for a couple of years
- Worked with the All Americans for a couple of years, under Jack Clark
- Organized some clinics with Jack Clark, Dennis Storer, Dale Toohey and Ray Cornbill
- Toured as Team Physician with Grizzlies to South Africa

- Listened carefully to Eddie O'Sullivan at George Hook's course at Colby College
- Went to New Zealand, to the Most Promising Young Players Camp, as an absorbent observer
- USA Rugby Level I coaching clinic, Portland, OR
- Wrote a well-received four-part series published in <u>Rugby</u> magazine, in 1984, on Teaching the Game (For Ed Hagerty, RIP)

Coached at San Diego State, with Steve Gray. Record 112-13-1 with 1987 National Championship

Coached University of San Diego, with something over 100 wins and an undefeated Southern California Collegiate season

Coached at USNA under Mike Flanagan with the men, then head coach for the women, with three final four appearances

Hall of Fame with the undefeated UCLA 1972 side (Not a starter)

Hall of fame, Loyola University, Evergreen, Baltimore, Maryland

Hall of Fame, San Diego State University, with the 1987 National Champions

Hall of Fame, University of San Diego

Proud presenter of the first two women Rugby Hall of Fame inductees at the United States Naval Academy

Four kids, 6 grandkids.

www.ingramcontent.com/pod-product-compliance
Lightning Source LLC
LaVergne TN
LVHW041625070526
838199LV00052B/3243